MIXED
METAPHORS
IDIOMS EXPOSED!

FACTOR OF FIVE USEFUL BOOKS

Title: Mixed Metaphors
Publisher: Factor of Five Useful Books
ISBN: 978-1-7644199-1-8
First published: 2025

A Cataloguing-in-Publication (CIP) record for this title is available from the National Library of Australia. Additional cataloguing records may be available from national libraries in other jurisdictions.

This publication is intended for international distribution. It is published in Australia and is compliant with Australian, UK, and U.S. copyright conventions.

Cover Design: Jane Fender Special Projects

Contents   Page

1.

A bird in the hand is worth two in the bush.

Better to hold on to something you already have than to risk losing it while chasing something uncertain. A reminder to value what's certain over speculative gains.

....

2.

Don't count your chickens before they hatch.

Don't assume success or make plans based on outcomes that haven't happened yet. Originates from farm life, where not every egg produces a chick.

....

3.

Fair dinkum.

A quintessentially Australian term meaning genuine, honest, or true. It reflects the cultural value placed on authenticity and straightforwardness.

....

4.

Bite off more than you can chew.

To take on more than you can realistically manage. A warning against over-commitment or overestimating your capacity.

....

5.

The early bird catches the worm.

Those who act early or take initiative are more likely to succeed. Encourages promptness and diligence.

....

6.

You can lead a horse to water, but you can't make it drink.

You can offer opportunities or advice, but you can't force someone to take them if they're unwilling.

....

7.

Every cloud has a silver lining.

Even difficult situations often have a hidden benefit or lesson. A call for optimism in adversity.

....

8.

Throw another shrimp on the barbie.

A phrase made famous internationally by advertising rather than everyday Australian speech. Represents friendly hospitality and the laid-back outdoor lifestyle.

....

9.

Good on ya.

An informal Australian expression of praise or congratulations. Equivalent to "well done".

....

10.

Like a kangaroo in the headlights.

Frozen in fear or surprise, unable to react, an Aussie variation on "like a deer in the headlights".

....

11.

Cutting corners.

Doing something in the quickest or cheapest way at the expense of quality or fairness. Suggests taking shortcuts that compromise standards.

....

12.

Burning the candle at both ends.

Working too hard or too long, to the point of exhaustion. Implies an unsustainable pace.

....

13.

A penny for your thoughts.

A polite way of asking someone what they're thinking,
implying their thoughts are valuable or interesting.

....

14.

All bark and no bite.

Describes someone who talks tough but rarely follows
through. Empty threats without real action.

....

15.

Beat around the bush.

Avoiding the main topic or issue. Derived from hunters who
beat bushes to flush out game but delayed facing it directly.

....

16.

Caught between a rock and a hard place.

In a dilemma with two unpleasant or difficult choices
and no easy escape.

....

17.

Don't put all your eggs in one basket.

Don't rely entirely on a single plan, investment, or source. Spreading risk provides security.

....

18.

Hit the nail on the head.

To be exactly right or perfectly accurate in identifying a problem or solution.

....

19.

Out of the frying pan into the fire.

Moving from a bad situation into one that's even worse, often by acting hastily.

....

20.

When it rains, it pours.

Troubles (or sometimes blessings) often arrive all at once rather than singly.

....

21.

Keep your chin up.

Stay positive and resilient in tough times. A physical metaphor for courage and confidence.

....

22.

Throw caution to the wind.

Act boldly or recklessly without worrying about possible risks or consequences.

....

23.

An apple a day keeps the doctor away.

Good health habits, especially eating nutritious food, help prevent illness.

....

24.

You can't teach an old dog new tricks.

It's hard to change long-established habits or convince people to adopt new ways.

....

25.

The pot calling the kettle black.

Accusing someone of a fault you share yourself; hypocrisy.

....

26.

A stitch in time saves nine.

Fix a small problem early to prevent it becoming a bigger one later.

....

27.

Bite the bullet.

Face a painful or unavoidable situation with courage. Originates from soldiers biting bullets to endure pain before anaesthesia existed.

....

28.

Break the ice.

Do or say something to reduce tension or awkwardness when people first meet.

....

29.

Close but no cigar.

Almost successful but not quite there; a near miss.

....

30.

Cry over spilt milk.

Regretting something that can't be undone is pointless—
move on and focus ahead.

....

31.

Every nook and cranny.

Every part or corner of something, no matter how
small or hidden. Used to describe a thorough search
or complete coverage.

....

32.

Full steam ahead.

To proceed with determination and maximum effort. Drawn
from steam engines running at full power, it suggests
momentum and commitment.

....

33.

Go against the grain.

To act contrary to what's expected or natural.
Often refers to behaviour that opposes convention,
habit, or one's own inclinations.

....

34.

Have an axe to grind.

To have a personal motive or hidden agenda behind one's
actions or opinions. Suggests that a person's contribution
isn't entirely objective.

....

35.

In seventh heaven.

To be in a state of pure joy, delight, or bliss.
Derived from ancient cosmology, where the seventh heaven
was the highest and most divine.

....

36.

Keep at bay.

To prevent something undesirable—like danger, illness, or
enemies—from getting too close or gaining ground.

....

37.

Let the cat out of the bag.

To reveal a secret, often accidentally. Originates from old market practices where a piglet in a sack might be dishonestly swapped for a cat.

....

38.

Make waves.

To cause a stir or disruption; to challenge the status quo. While sometimes negative, it can also describe someone initiating meaningful change.

....

39.

Leave no stone unturned.

To search thoroughly or explore every possibility in pursuit of a goal. Encourages persistence and diligence.

....

40.

Play it by ear.

To handle a situation spontaneously rather than following a fixed plan. Draws from music—playing without written notes.

....

41.

Queer the pitch.

To spoil or disrupt someone's plans, usually in a subtle or underhanded way. Originally a theatrical term meaning to ruin a performance.

....

42.

Run the gamut.

To cover the full range or spectrum of something. From "gamut," meaning the entire musical scale.

....

43.

Stick to your guns.

To maintain one's opinion or position despite criticism or opposition. Suggests courage and conviction in the face of pressure.

....

44.

Turn a blind eye.

To deliberately ignore something wrong or inconvenient. Originates from Admiral Nelson, who supposedly raised his telescope to his blind eye to avoid seeing a signal to retreat.

....

45.

Up for grabs.

Available to anyone who wants to claim or compete for it.
Implies an open opportunity.

....

46.

Vie for attention.

To compete with others for notice, praise, or recognition.

....

47.

Wipe the slate clean.

To forget past problems or mistakes and start afresh. Comes
from chalk slates once used for writing and easily erased.

....

48.

A storm in a teacup.

A small issue exaggerated out of proportion.
Popular in British English, suggesting drama
brewed in a very tiny vessel.

....

49.

Zip your lip.

To stop talking or keep quiet, often used when confidentiality or silence is required.

....

50.

Add fuel to the fire.

To make a bad situation worse by saying or doing something provocative. Emphasises escalation.

....

51.

Caught red-handed.

To be discovered in the act of wrongdoing. The phrase originates from being found literally with blood on one's hands.

....

52.

Down and out.

To be destitute or lacking resources, often both financially and emotionally defeated.

....

53.

An eye for an eye.

A call for retributive justice, repaying a wrong with an equal act. Comes from ancient legal codes such as Hammurabi's law.

....

54.

Find your bearings.

To work out where you are or what direction to take, physically or metaphorically. Implies orientation and clarity.

....

55.

Give the cold shoulder.

To deliberately ignore or snub someone. Believed to come from offering guests a cold meal to signal they'd overstayed their welcome.

....

56.

Hit below the belt.

To act unfairly or unethically, especially in argument or competition. Drawn from boxing, where blows below the beltline are illegal.

....

57.

Jump the shark.

To reach the point where something—especially a TV show or trend—declines in quality after a gimmick or desperate attempt to stay relevant. Originates from Happy Days, when Fonzie literally jumped a shark on water-skis.

....

58.

The last straw.

The final irritation or problem in a series that pushes someone to their limit. Comes from the saying "the straw that broke the camel's back."

....

59.

Meet your match.

To encounter someone equal or superior in skill or strength, often unexpectedly.

....

60.

Not hold water.

A theory, excuse, or argument that doesn't stand up to scrutiny—figuratively "leaking" like a faulty vessel.

....

61.

On the dot.

Exactly on time; punctual to the precise minute.
Often used when meetings or events start precisely as
scheduled.

....

62.

Pull out all the stops.

To use every available resource or effort to achieve
something impressive. Originates from pipe organs, where
pulling out the "stops" allows maximum sound.

....

63.

Quick on the draw.

Able to react or respond quickly, especially in conversation or
competition. Comes from the speed of drawing a gun in old
Westerns.

....

64.

Ride out the storm.

To endure or survive a difficult situation until it passes. Drawn
from seafaring language—weathering a literal storm at sea.

....

65.

Sell someone short.

To underestimate someone's abilities or potential.
Also used in finance, but colloquially means failing to
recognise someone's full value.

....

66.

Take the cake.

To be the best, or sometimes the worst, of a particular group.
Historically linked to winning a cake as a prize in competitions.

....

67.

Under the wire.

To finish or achieve something just in time.
Derived from horse racing, where competitors cross
the wire at the finish line.

....

68.

Voice in the wilderness.

A lone person expressing a warning or opinion that few
others heed. Comes from biblical imagery of prophets calling
out in desolate places.

....

69.

Wash your hands of it.

To refuse further involvement or responsibility. Originates from Pontius Pilate symbolically washing his hands to show detachment from an execution decision.

....

70.

X marks the spot.

Indicates the exact location, often used humorously or in reference to treasure maps.

....

71.

Chicken out.

To lose nerve or back out of something daunting at the last moment. The comparison to a timid chicken has been used for centuries to describe fear.

....

72.

Zero hour.

The exact scheduled time when an operation or significant event is set to begin, often used in military contexts.

....

73.

Across the board.

Affecting everyone or everything equally; universal in scope.

....

74.

Bite your tongue.

To stop yourself from saying something you might regret. Suggests self-restraint in speech.

....

75.

Clear the air.

To resolve tension or misunderstanding by discussing things openly. Often used after arguments or disagreements.

....

76.

Draw the short straw.

To be chosen—by chance—for an unpleasant or undesirable task. Based on the literal act of drawing lots.

....

77.

Eat your words.

To admit you were wrong about something you said. Usually follows being proven mistaken.

....

78.

For all intents and purposes.

In every practical sense, effectively. Sometimes misquoted as "for all intents and purposes."

....

79.

Get the ball rolling.

To begin an activity or process. Evokes the image of starting motion that continues on its own momentum.

....

80.

Have the upper hand.

To be in a position of control or advantage. Possibly derived from wrestling, where having one's hand above the opponent provides leverage.

....

81.

In the driver's seat.

To be in charge or in control of a situation. Comes from the literal act of steering a vehicle.

....

82.

Keep your shirt on.

A friendly way to tell someone to calm down or be patient. Stemming from a time when removing one's shirt implied readiness for a fight.

....

83.

Live and let live.

To tolerate others' differences and expect the same in return. A principle of mutual respect and coexistence.

....

84.

Move mountains.

To achieve something extraordinary or seemingly impossible. Suggests determination and faith overcoming huge obstacles.

....

85.

Never say die.

An encouragement to persevere; to never give up hope despite setbacks.

....

86.

Open a can of worms.

To start a complicated problem or situation that becomes difficult to control.

....

87.

Put your foot in your mouth.

To say something embarrassing, tactless, or inappropriate without meaning to.

....

88.

Keep something at arm's length.

To maintain distance, emotionally, physically, or strategically. Comes from keeping a sword-wielding opponent just far enough away to avoid danger.

....

89.

Rub salt in the wound.

To make a bad or painful situation worse by adding further insult or injury.

....

90.

See eye to eye.

To agree completely or share the same view as someone else.

....

91.

Through thick and thin.

To stay loyal or committed regardless of circumstances. Suggests enduring both good times ("thick") and bad ("thin").

....

92.

Under the gun.

Feeling intense pressure to meet a deadline or perform under stress. Evokes being figuratively "held at gunpoint" by time or expectation.

....

93.

Vicious cycle.

A sequence of events where one problem leads to another, reinforcing and worsening the first.

....

94.

Walk the plank.

To face punishment or take the consequences of one's actions. Originates from pirate lore, where offenders were forced off a plank into the sea.

....

95.

You're toast.

A colloquial expression meaning you're in serious trouble or about to face consequences.

....

96.

Zip it.

To stop talking immediately; to be quiet. A modern, informal variant of "zip your lip."

....

97.

Add insult to injury.

To make a bad situation worse by adding an extra layer of harm or offence.

....

98.

His bark is worse than his bite.

Describes someone who seems aggressive or threatening but is actually harmless or gentle in action.

....

99.

Cut someone some slack.

To be lenient or forgiving towards someone; to ease up on criticism or pressure.

....

100.

Don't rock the boat.

To avoid causing trouble or disrupting the status quo. From the idea that rocking a boat can make it unstable.

....

101.

Eye of the storm.

The calm centre of chaos or conflict. In meteorology, the eye of a cyclone is the still area surrounded by turbulent winds.

....

102.

Fight tooth and nail.

To struggle fiercely for something,
using every possible effort or advantage.

....

103.

Go for broke.

To risk everything on a single attempt. Popularised by gambling and later by military usage.

....

104.

Hit the books.

To study seriously and with focus.
Commonly used among students.

....

105.

In a pickle.

In a difficult or awkward situation.
The phrase dates back to Shakespeare, who used it to
describe being in a "sour" predicament.

....

106.

Jump through hoops.

To go through a series of unnecessary or demanding
procedures to achieve something. From circus imagery of
animals trained to jump through hoops.

....

107.

Knock it out of the park.

To do something exceptionally well or successfully. Comes
from baseball, meaning a home run.

....

108.

Last-ditch effort.

A final, desperate attempt to succeed after all
other options have failed. Originates from military
terminology, defending the last ditch.

....

109.

Make a beeline for.

To head directly and quickly towards something or someone. Inspired by the straight path bees take when returning to their hive.

....

110.

Not all it's cracked up to be.

Something that doesn't live up to its reputation or expectations.

....

111.

Off the record.

Information shared in confidence, not intended for public release or attribution. Common in journalism and politics.

....

112.

Play your cards right.

To use your resources or opportunities wisely in order to succeed. Comes from card games and strategy.

....

113.

Question of judgement.

A situation where a decision depends on personal interpretation, wisdom, or moral reasoning rather than strict rules.

....

114.

Ruffle feathers.

To annoy or upset people by saying or doing something that disturbs harmony. Draws from the image of a bird with its feathers unsettled.

....

115.

Steal the show.

To attract the most attention or praise, often unexpectedly. Typically used for performers or standout contributors.

....

116.

Tip of the iceberg.

A small visible part of a much larger hidden problem. Refers to how most of an iceberg lies beneath the water's surface.

....

117.

Up the ante.

To increase the stakes, demands, or intensity in a situation. Derived from poker, where players raise their bets.

....

118.

Venture into the unknown.

To explore or attempt something new without knowing what lies ahead. Suggests courage and discovery.

....

119.

Weather the storm.

To endure a period of difficulty until it passes. A seafaring metaphor for resilience.

....

120.

Xenial hospitality.

Displaying warm, generous hospitality towards guests or strangers. Derived from the ancient Greek concept of xenia, meaning sacred guest-friendship.

....

121.

Not playing with a full deck.

A humorous way of saying someone is acting irrationally or missing crucial information. Refers to a deck of cards missing pieces, making the game impossible.

....

122.

Zero-sum game.

When one person's gain is exactly balanced by another's loss with no overall benefit. Common in economics and competitive strategy.

....

123.

Across the aisle.

To cooperate or negotiate with people from an opposing side, particularly in politics or business. Derived from the physical aisle dividing parliamentary benches.

....

124.

Break new ground.

To do something innovative or unprecedented. Drawn from agriculture, turning over soil that hasn't been cultivated before.

....

125.

Come full circle.

To return to an original position, situation, or mindset after a journey or series of changes. Implies a sense of completion or inevitability.

....

126.

Dodge a bullet.

To narrowly avoid a serious problem, danger, or disaster. Originates from literal gunfire but is now used figuratively.

....

127.

Elbow grease.

Hard physical work or effort. A humorous way of saying something requires manual labour rather than luck or talent.

....

128.

Feather in one's cap.

An achievement or honour to be proud of. Based on the old practice of adding feathers to a cap as marks of accomplishment.

....

129.

Go out on a limb.

To take a risk or make a bold statement, often to support someone or something. Comes from climbing onto a fragile branch that could break.

....

130.

Hedge your bets.

To reduce risk by supporting more than one option or strategy. Borrowed from betting language.

....

131.

In the loop.

To be kept informed and involved in ongoing discussions or decisions. Implies being part of an inner circle of communication.

....

132.

Jump at the chance.

To eagerly seize an opportunity without hesitation.

....

133.

Keep your cool.

To stay calm under pressure or provocation.

....

134.

Lose track of time.

To become so absorbed in an activity that you're unaware of how much time has passed.

....

135.

Make headway.

To make progress towards a goal, particularly when it's slow or difficult. A nautical metaphor referring to a ship moving forward through resistance.

....

136.

Nail your colours to the mast.

To publicly declare one's position or beliefs and refuse to back down. Originates from naval battles, where lowering the flag signalled surrender.

....

137.

Off the grid.

Living independently of public utilities such as electricity and water, or metaphorically, outside conventional systems or social visibility.

....

138.

Pave the way.

To create the conditions that make progress or success easier for others. Derived from literally paving a smoother road for travel.

....

139.

Raise the bar.

To set a higher standard or level of expectation. Comes from high jumping and athletics, where the bar is raised for each new attempt.

....

140.

Sink or swim.

To succeed or fail entirely through one's own effort. Reflects the idea of being thrown into water and forced to either adapt or drown.

....

141.

Turn the tide.

To cause a significant change in circumstances or outcomes, especially from negative to positive. A maritime image of shifting current direction.

....

142.

Under wraps.

To keep something secret, private, or hidden until the right time.

....

143.

Voice of reason.

A person who provides calm, sensible advice in an emotional or chaotic situation.

....

144.

Wring your hands.

To show worry or distress without taking useful action. The image comes from the physical act of twisting one's hands together in anxiety.

....

145.

Jump on the bandwagon.

To join a trend or movement simply because it's popular. Originates from 19th-century parade wagons that attracted crowds and supporters.

....

146.

Zigzag path.

A route that twists and turns rather than going straight, often used metaphorically for a process full of challenges or detours.

....

147.

Keeping up with the Joneses.

To compete with neighbours or peers in social status or possessions. Highlights material comparison and social pressure.

....

148.

Putting all your cards on the table.

Being fully honest and transparent about your intentions or position. Comes from card games where revealing your hand removes all secrecy.

....

149.

Moving the needle.

Creating a noticeable impact or measurable change in performance or results.

....

150.

Not seeing the forest for the trees.

Focusing too much on details and losing sight of the bigger picture. A metaphor for narrow or overly literal thinking.

....

151.

Opening the kimono.

To reveal confidential or sensitive information, often in a business context. The phrase implies transparency during negotiations or partnerships, though it's now used cautiously due to cultural sensitivity.

....

152.

Someone who appears harmless but has harmful intentions. Stems from biblical imagery of predators disguising themselves among the flock.

....

153.

Quarterbacking.

To lead or coordinate a team or project by directing actions and making key decisions. Drawn from American football, where the quarterback guides the play.

....

154.

Ringing the cash register.

To generate sales or profit. Used figuratively to describe successful commercial results.

....

155.

The Bark is peeling off the tree.

Signals something is going wrong on the surface before deeper issues emerge. Drawn from forestry, where peeling bark indicates disease or stress.

....

156.

Table stakes.

The minimum requirements needed to compete in a particular market or situation. From poker, where players must place a basic bet to enter the game.

....

157.

Unicorn.

A startup company valued at over one billion dollars, typically in the tech industry. The term reflects rarity and exceptional success.

....

158.

Leave someone high and dry.

To abandon someone in a difficult situation with no support. Nautical in origin—ships stranded on low tide were literally left "high and dry."

....

159.

White elephant.

An expensive or burdensome possession that's more trouble than it's worth. Originates from the legend of the sacred white elephants of Siam, which bankrupted their owners due to upkeep costs.

....

160.

X-efficiency.

A term from economics referring to efficiency achieved by minimising waste and maximising productivity beyond theoretical limits.

....

161.

Yellow pad session.

An informal brainstorming meeting, named after the classic yellow legal pad often used for jotting ideas.

....

162.

A watched pot never boils..

Waiting impatiently makes time feel slower and progress seem invisible. From the kitchen truth that constant watching never makes the boil arrive sooner.

....

163.

Cash cow.

A reliable source of steady profit requiring little effort to maintain. Commonly used for established products or services that fund other ventures.

....

164.

Elevator pitch.

A concise, persuasive summary of an idea, product, or business, short enough to deliver during a brief elevator ride.

....

165.

Frictionless market.

An idealised market where transactions occur effortlessly without barriers, delays, or costs.

....

166.

Golden handshake.

A generous payment or benefits package given to an employee, often upon early retirement or redundancy.

....

167.

Hockey stick growth.

A pattern showing slow initial progress followed by a sharp rise, resembling the shape of a hockey stick. Commonly used to describe startup growth curves.

....

168.

Influencer marketing.

Promoting products through individuals who have credibility and large followings, especially on social media.

....

169.

Just-in-time (JIT) inventory.

A supply management method where materials are ordered and received only as needed, reducing waste and storage costs.

....

170.

Knowledge economy.

An economy driven by information, innovation, and expertise rather than traditional industries like manufacturing or agriculture.

....

171.

Low-hanging fruit.

Tasks or opportunities that are easy to achieve or yield quick results. Suggests prioritising simple wins before tackling complex challenges.

....

172.

Swimming with sharks.

Operating in a highly competitive or dangerous environment. Highlights the risks of dealing with aggressive or predatory individuals.

....

173.

Moving the goalposts.

Changing the criteria or objectives after a process has started, often unfairly.

....

174.

On the same page.

Having a shared understanding or agreement about a plan, idea, or goal.

....

175.

Pushing the envelope.

To go beyond normal limits or expectations. Originates from aviation, referring to testing an aircraft's performance boundaries.

....

176.

Thinking outside the box.

Approaching problems creatively, beyond conventional thinking.

....

177.

At a crossroads.

Facing a crucial decision point that will determine future direction. Comes from the literal image of choosing a path at an intersection.

....

178.

Burning the midnight oil.

Working late into the night. From a time when oil lamps were used for light during long hours of study or labour.

....

179.

Climbing the corporate ladder.

Advancing step by step through the hierarchy of an organisation. Implies ambition and steady professional growth.

....

180.

Barking up the wrong tree.

Pursuing the wrong person, solution, or assumption. Originates from hunting dogs who would mistakenly bark at the base of the wrong tree, believing their prey was there.

....

181.

Dropping the ball.

To fail to carry out a responsibility or complete a task properly. Comes from ball games where losing control of the ball signifies failure.

....

182.

Fishing for compliments.

To seek praise or validation indirectly, often by pretending modesty or self-doubt.

....

183.

Getting the green light.

Receiving approval or permission to proceed with a plan or project. Drawn from traffic signals meaning "go."

....

184.

Hitting the ground running.

To begin a new task or role energetically and effectively, without delay or adjustment time.

....

185.

The ball is in your court.

It's your turn to take action or make a decision. Borrowed from tennis, where possession of the ball dictates responsibility for the next move.

....

186.

Juggling too many balls.

Managing multiple tasks or responsibilities at once, often leading to stress or mistakes. Evokes a literal juggler at risk of dropping something.

....

187.

Keeping your ear to the ground.

To stay alert to new trends, news, or developments. Comes from the old practice of listening to vibrations through the ground to detect approaching footsteps or horses.

....

188.

Level playing field.

A fair and equal environment where everyone has the same opportunity to succeed. Common in sport and business contexts.

....

189.

Money talks.

The idea that financial power influences decisions and outcomes more effectively than words or principles.

....

190.

Navigating through choppy waters.

Managing through a period of difficulty or uncertainty. Drawn from sailing imagery of rough seas.

....

191.

Bite the hand that feeds you.

To harm or betray someone who has helped or supported you. Evokes the image of an animal turning on the person providing its food.

....

192.

Peeling back the onion.

Analysing a problem layer by layer to uncover its deeper causes. Suggests complexity beneath the surface.

....

193.

Quick win.

An easily achievable success that delivers immediate positive results, often used to build momentum.

....

194.

Throw your hat in the ring.

To volunteer or enter a competition or candidacy. Comes from old boxing matches where contenders signalled their entry by tossing a hat into the ring.

....

195.

Sealing the deal.

To finalise an agreement or contract.
Derived from the traditional act of sealing a document with wax as formal confirmation.

....

196.

Thinking on your feet.

To make quick decisions or respond effectively in the moment, especially under pressure.

....

197.

Under the radar.

To operate quietly or unnoticed,
avoiding public attention or scrutiny.

....

198.

Value proposition.

The unique set of benefits or advantages offered by a
product, service, or organisation that differentiates
it from competitors.

....

199.

Win-win situation.

An outcome that benefits all parties involved, with no losers.
Common in negotiation or collaboration contexts.

....

200.

Go down in flames.

To fail spectacularly rather than gradually. Inspired by
aircraft disasters where the descent is dramatic and
irreversible.

....

201.

Bend over backwards.

To go to great lengths or make extraordinary effort to help someone. Suggests an unnatural contortion made willingly for another's sake.

....

202.

The elephant in the room.

An obvious issue everyone sees but avoids addressing. The metaphor highlights how something huge and impossible to ignore can still go unspoken.

....

203.

Breaking the glass ceiling.

Overcoming invisible barriers that prevent advancement— particularly for women and minorities in professional hierarchies.

....

204.

Change agent.

A person who initiates or drives significant transformation within an organisation.

....

205.

Ducks in a row.

To be well-organised and prepared before
taking action. Likely derived from the neat alignment of
ducklings following their mother.

....

206.

Eating your own dog food.

To use your own company's products or services as
proof of confidence and quality. Common in technology and
product-development circles.

....

207.

Firing on all cylinders.

Operating at maximum efficiency and performance.
Comes from the mechanics of a fully functioning engine.

....

208.

Going the extra mile.

To make an exceptional effort beyond what is expected.
Derived from a biblical reference to Roman law, encouraging
generosity of spirit.

....

209.

Don't beat a dead horse.

To continue arguing a point or pursuing an issue long after it's no longer useful. Suggests futility, no amount of effort can revive what's already gone.

....

210.

In the trenches.

To be deeply involved in the hardest or most demanding parts of work. Drawn from soldiers working in literal battle trenches.

....

211.

Jumping ship.

To abandon a project, job, or organisation, especially when failure seems imminent. Comes from sailors literally leaving a sinking vessel.

....

212.

Burning bridges.

Damaging relationships or opportunities in a way that makes it hard to return. Draws from the military tactic of destroying bridges to prevent retreat.

....

213.

Closing thoughts.

While not a metaphor itself, this concluding note emphasises that idioms and metaphors shape how we express ambition, resilience, and failure. Mixed Metaphors celebrates that interplay—revealing not only what we say, but how our shared language reflects who we are.

....

214.

Carry the torch.

To continue supporting, believing in, or advocating for something passionately. Originally linked to torchbearers leading the way during ceremonies or battles.

....

215.

Let sleeping dogs lie.

Avoid revisiting old conflicts or stirring up issues that have already settled. Suggests that disturbing what's peaceful can create unnecessary trouble.

....

www.ingramcontent.com/pod-product-compliance
Lightning Source LLC
Chambersburg PA
CBHW070817280326
41934CB00012B/3205